THE MILLS & BOON®
MODERN GIRL'S GUIDE TO

Happy
Hour

HQ
An imprint of HarperCollinsPublishers Ltd.
1 London Bridge Street
London SE1 9GF

This hardback edition 2016

1
First published in Great Britain by
HQ, an imprint of HarperCollinsPublishers Ltd. 2016

A catalogue record for this book is
available from the British Library

ISBN: 978-0-00-821234-6

Printed and bound in Italy

Funny, feisty and feminist:
The Mills & Boon Modern Girl's Survival Guides.

Introduction

Girls, whatever the time of year, you can always be sure of one thing: Happy Hour is the most important time of day. It comes after work and before bed; that magical phase when you're both conscious and don't have to speak to Wendy from Sales.

The question is: where to spend yours? Should you Go Out and accept that guy from Tinder's invitation to take up The Duke's 2-4-1 Mojito offer (sure, you can see a 2010 calendar hanging up in his profile picture, but it's been a while)? Or should you return to the safety of your home and revel in me-time, flagrantly risking FOMO?

The unpalatable truth is that, whether you enjoy your Happy Hour inside or outside, there's so much pressure to have fun that it will probably be terrible. Sure, inside has Netflix, duvets and giant plates of biscuits. But inside also has those lemons you've been meaning to throw away for a month, crushing ennui and the inevitability of dying alone. Meanwhile, outside has art installations and vitamin D. But outside also has the weather, adults on little scooters designed for children and taxi drivers telling you their opinions.

Unfortunately, you can't just hover awkwardly in a door halfway between the two your entire life but, reader, you are in luck. Welcome to The A-Z of Happy Hour: the definitive guide to having fun (or at least pretending to).

Alcohol

It doesn't count towards your weekly tally if you drink it out of a teacup in front of Bargain Hunt.

I read that in a book.

Battery woes

Janine, Estelle and Matilda have been friends for a long time.

So it was even more unsettling when they discovered that the time between 'phone battery dying' and 'reverting to a semi-barbaric Upper Palaeolithic state where cannibalism is very much an option being considered' was slightly less than half an hour.

Beach Body Ready

Oh, sorry, pal, was 'ready to lure you to a watery death, bashed to bits against these desolate craggy rocks', not the type of 'ready' you were banging on about?

Shame.

Cards

Card Games Suitable For The Modern Woman:

Jacks and Kings Earn Double

Queens Pay Tampon Tax

Solitaire Is Fine Actually, I'm Over You, Gavin

Patience

Culture

Beth has resolved to broaden her outlook.
She has decided to give groundbreaking
experimental theatre a chance.

Beth has made a terrible mistake.

Drunk eBay

There was a point, somewhere around 1 a.m. and the second bottle of gin, when it had suddenly seemed really important to Abi that she should order a hundred and fifteen identical Channing Tatum plastic figurines.

But now, in the cold light of day, with the postman giving her one of his looks, she couldn't one hundred per cent remember why that had been the case.

Designated Driver

Minnie is practising her driving skills
with her best friend.

They are both having lots of fun.

Driving will become less fun when Minnie discovers
that, due to a rare genetic condition, she is allergic
to alcohol, and will spend the rest of her life giving
lifts to people who are too drunk to remember
where they live.

Figure 1:

Figure 2:

Expectations

Figure 1: What Jane hoped the guys at the party would be like.

Figure 2: The actual guys at the party.

Experiments

Scarlett's home science experiments had started off fun, but there was no sugar-coating the fact that this time they probably should have gone bowling.

Forgetting

Margot hasn't got a clue why she came in here.

Was it to . . . look at some feathers in a jar?

Smoke the rest of this cigarette?

Strike a weird sort of pose and think
about her lower back pain?

Oh God, this is happening more
and more often.

Friends

Linda and Simone are going to a party.

Linda is going to keep an eye on her pedometer and tell Simone when they have danced enough to leave and get doner kebabs.

That's what friends are for.

Food

True, she hadn't baked before, and it's not what the recipe said to do at all, but Phyllis just knew that if Paul Hollywood was here he'd approve of her decision to add an entire jar of honey to the sourdough mix.

'You've made a bold choice,' Paul would purr, fixing her with those piercing blue eyes. 'I admire that.'

Gallery

Possibly this is a performance piece questioning the subjugation of women artists in a patriarchal world.

Possibly it is just someone trying to steal the exhibit.

The important thing is to rub your chin and say, 'Of course, it puts me in mind of the French school's later proto-Bauhaus period.'

Or, if that fails, murmur something about man's inhumanity to man.

Hobbies

Fulfilling Activities That
Are Definitely Worth Doing:

Organising your collection of light
bulbs in order of size

Alphabetising the egg cups

Breadstick whittling

Getting into arguments in the comments
section of news websites

Having to Go

Linda is desperate for a wee.

But the queue for the loo was huge, so she's nipped outside to go behind a handy tree.

Unfortunately, the tree is on the smokers' terrace.

Home Perms

You know you shouldn't.

But somehow you have.

Hen-Do's

'L-Plates are patronising,' they said.

'Butlers in the buff are such a cliché,' they said.

'It's ironic,' they said.

Belinda couldn't help but wish she'd chosen
a more basic set of bridesmaids.

Invitations

A lot of people would be upset not to get a Facebook invite to Chloe's party.

But not Janine.

Janine has a fun hobby weighing tiny dogs. Weighing tiny dogs is actually very important.

Janine doesn't need any of you. She doesn't.

Impulse Buy

Olivia only came out for a pint of milk, but these fireproof, noiseless false teeth come with a ten-day free trial.

Olivia will lose the receipt and spend the rest of her life feeling guilty whenever she accidentally finds the teeth in the back of her cutlery drawer.

Jigsaws

On the one hand, realising there was a piece of her Doctor Who jigsaw missing wasn't as bad as realising that doing Doctor Who jigsaws on a Friday night meant there was a missing piece of her *life*.

On the other hand, perhaps it was *worse*, because it meant Peter Capaldi only had half a face.

Karaoke

Denise and John's go-to choice for a karaoke evening is the whole of Wagner's Ring Cycle, sung in the style of an angry Avril Lavigne.

Denise and John are not popular.

Liquor Cabinet

Seventeen years ago, Francine cleared out her grandmother's liquor cabinet and kept back a bottle of Chartreuse and a case of Cherry Bs.

Today, it is 11:03 p.m. The supermarket has closed, and Francine has been swiping right for three hours.

Francine is calling this drink *The Ad Nauseous*.

Museums

Chrissie knew she shouldn't have let her dad choose
the venue for meeting her new boyfriend.

She wishes he would admit that The Pencil Museum
was a mistake and let them go to the pub.

Netflix And Chill

An evening of Gavin doing the old 'yawn and stretch' routine then trying to 'accidentally' unhook her bra hardly seemed worth it once Rita realised Netflix didn't even have season eight of *RuPaul's Drag Race*.

Outdoors

Reasons To Go Outdoors:

There are dogs.

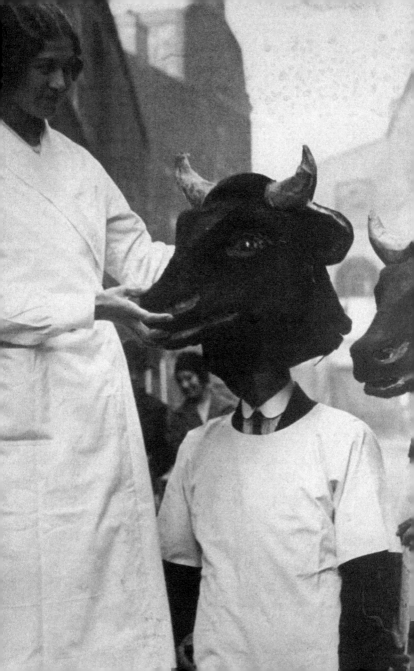

Papier Mâché

Esme has quit her job as a careers guidance counsellor and opened an Etsy shop selling papier mâché heads.

The irony is lost on Esme.

Partying

Alma was having the time of her life until the lights came on and she realised that she was the oldest person in *Infernos* by at least a decade.

Pinterest

Today was the day Liz decided to make
all her pins a reality.

Quiz

She'd said 'Canberra' six times.

But Colin had the pen, and apparently 'having the pen' means you get to overrule the person who lived in Australia for a decade based on 'a very strong hunch that it's Sydney'.

Colin won't be taking another quiz any time soon.

Rear Window

Look, it's Doris from number nineteen, and that's definitely not her Frank paying a visit at this time in the afternoon, is it?

And there's Terence from round the corner, wearing the very same outfit he went out in last night. I'm saying nothing - you can draw your own conclusions.

Basically, I'm exactly the same as Jimmy Stewart in Rear Window. You'll thank me if a murder needs solving.

Street Harassment

Andrea gets a lot of unwanted street
harassment when she goes out.

But it's probably her own fault for wearing the kind
of outfits that show off almost her entire hand and
can only withstand gas attacks for up to six hours.

Sibling Rivalry

You have tried to bankrupt yourself three times.

A stint in jail is looking attractive.

You wish you were at a real train station,
with a one-way ticket to anywhere.

If George doesn't land on your hotel soon you are
either going to stove his head in with a miniature
iron or make him swallow that little metal dog.

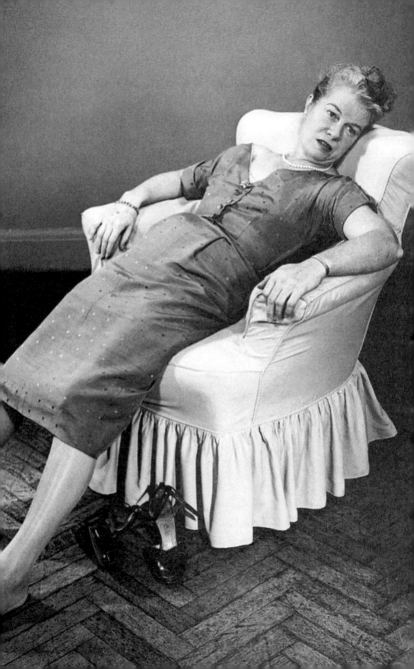

Televison Binge

Elsie wasn't sure how she had gone from 'it's OK to watch another hour of this' to 'it's OK to have not eaten anything apart from this bag of Frazzles for a day now' to 'it's OK to have developed all these bedsores' to 'it's OK to have missed Frank's graduation', but one more episode wasn't going to hurt at this point.

Terrible Restaurants

Rejected ideas for hipster eateries that will nonetheless probably happen within five years anyway:

Bring Your Own Pigs!

Lobsters In The Dark

Imaginary Ham

Hooves, Any Which Way

Up-Cycling

Kelly started a blog on the joys of up-cycling before realising she has no actual clue how to up-cycle stuff.

Now she has to wear this stupid monster lampshade as a hat all the time in the hope that it counts.

Vamoose

Apparently the next stop on the girls' night out was an underground tattoo parlour.

Annie had hoped to make a quiet getaway, but things haven't gone quite to plan.

Ventriloquism

Christine is convinced that making a hand puppet out of old socks and some make-up removal pads then having conversations with it about what they are going to have for tea will get her a spot on Britain's Got Talent.

But Christine has been 'practising' for three years now and even Colin the monkey isn't convinced that this is going anywhere.

Womanhood

'Don't let your period get in the way of your inner goddess!', this Tampon commercial proclaims.

Nora would probably Tweet something sarcastic
if she wasn't doubled up in agony on the sofa,
surrounded by her emergency supply of heavy-flow
sanitary towels and half-eaten boxes of Milk Tray.

Xmas Parties

After the unmentionable events of 2015,
the open bar at this year's office Christmas party
ran to half a pint each.

Everyone is desperate to go home.

Yawn

There are Buddhist monks who practise for years to get to the serene state of not having a single thought trouble their brains.

This is a state that Doris is able to reach with increasing ease, usually within about three minutes of sitting down to write her important novel.

Zoo

Reasons I Am No Longer
Welcome At The Local Zoo:

Petting the ostrich despite signs to the contrary

Trying to use the ostrich as a cheap
alternative to hailing a cab

My Ostrich surge pricing policy

About Ada Adverse

Ada was brought up in a deeply puritanical household where looking at a cake or using words containing more than one vowel were considered decadences punishable by a night in the coal cellar. But at fifteen she ran away from home and is now the world's leading authority on Having Fun, which is definitely an actual job. She has 'Fungineer' printed on her business cards to prove it, though in retrospect she should have been more clear that this does not mean she specialises in mushrooms.

Ada's hobbies include topiary, mazes, homing pigeons, flea circuses, forming imaginary bands in her head, embalming things, tattoos, pylons, and the films of Billy Wilder.

Ada's dislikes include predatory macaws, getting out the wrong side of the bed, collections of masks, and porcelain dolls with realistic teeth.

About Mills & Boon®

Since 1908, Mills & Boon have been a girl's best friend.

We've seen a lot change in the years since: enjoying sex as a woman is now not only officially fine but actively encouraged, dry shampoo has revolutionised our lives and, best of all, we've come full circle on gin.

But being a woman still has its challenges. We're under-paid, exhaustingly objectified, and under-represented at top tables. We work for free from 19th November, and our life-choices are scrutinised and forever found lacking. Plus: PMS; unsolicited d*ck pics; the price of tights.

Sometimes, a girl just needs a break.
And, for a century, that's where we've come in.

So, to celebrate one hundred years of wisdom (or at least a lot of fun), we've produced these handy A-Zs: funny, feisty, feminist guides to help the modern girl get through the day.

We can't promise an end to the bullsh*t.
But we can offer some light relief along the way.